SCHIRMER'S LIBRARY
OF MUSICAL CLASSICS

Vol. 1816

Julius Klengel

Technical Studies

For the Violoncello

G. SCHIRMER, Inc.

DISTRIBUTED BY

HAL•LEONARD®
CORPORATION
7777 W. BLUEMOUND RD. P.O. BOX 13819 MILWAUKEE, WI 53213

Printed in the U.S.A.

Foreword to the First Edition

The undersigned decided to publish these studies at the request of his numerous pupils, although he realizes that many scale studies for the cello are already in existence. However, as there are many diverse opinions about the treatment of this most important, essential branch of teaching, the undersigned felt it appropriate to publish these studies, since they represent thirty years of teaching experience. As far as the undersigned knows, only he has so far used scales, triads and broken thirds through all the keys in such a persistent way; and from this point of view the publication of these exercises may have some justification.

Julius Klengel

Biographical Note

Klengel, Julius, German cellist; brother of Paul Klengel; born Leipzig, Sept. 24, 1859; died there, Oct. 27, 1933. Brought up in a musical atmosphere (virtually all members of his family were professional or amateur musicians), he developed rapidly; studied cello with Emil Hegar and theory with Jadassohn. He joined the Gewandhaus Orchestra in 1874, when he was 15; in 1881 he became 1st cellist, and remained in that post until his resignation in 1924. He also taught at the Leipzig Conservatory. He traveled widely in Europe as a soloist; composed a number of works for his instrument, among them 4 concertos; a *Konzertstück* for cello with piano; *Hymnus* for 12 cellos; a double concerto for violin and cello; and 2 string quartets and a piano trio; edited a number of cello works; published cello exercises.

Reprinted from *Baker's Biographical Dictionary of Musicians,* fifth edition, completely revised by Nicolas Slonimsky.

Table of Abbreviations

Fr.	=	frog of the bow
Pt.	=	point of the bow
M.	=	middle of the bow
W.B.	=	whole bow
M.Pt.	=	middle to the point
Pt.M.	=	point to the middle
Fr.M.	=	frog to the middle
M.Fr.	=	middle to the frog
⌐‾⌐	=	keep fingers down

TECHNICAL STUDIES
for Cello

Scales in two octaves

JULIUS KLENGEL

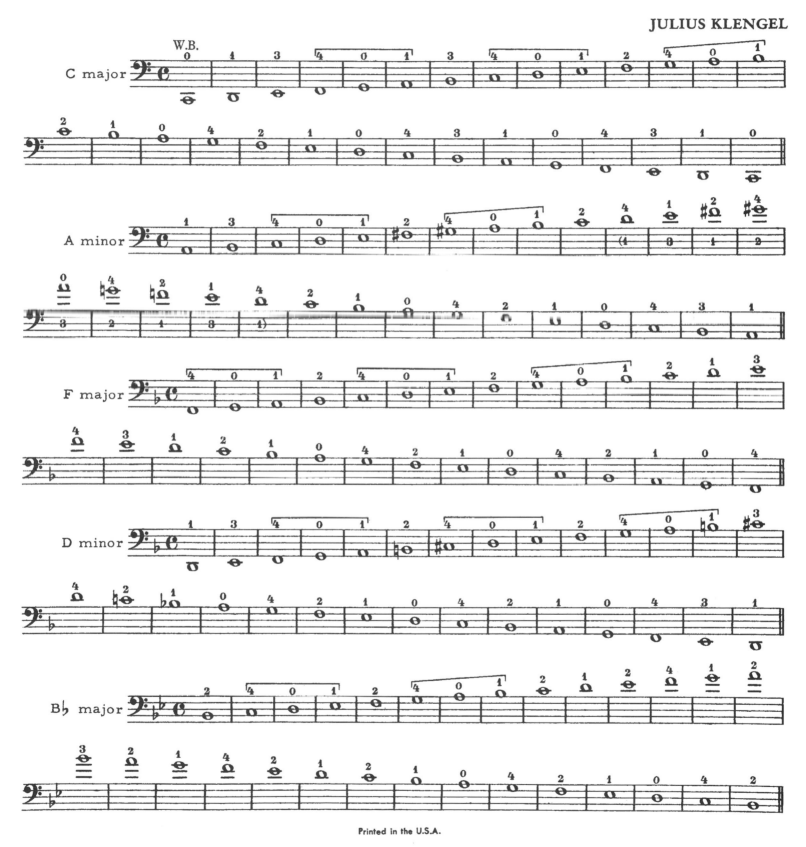

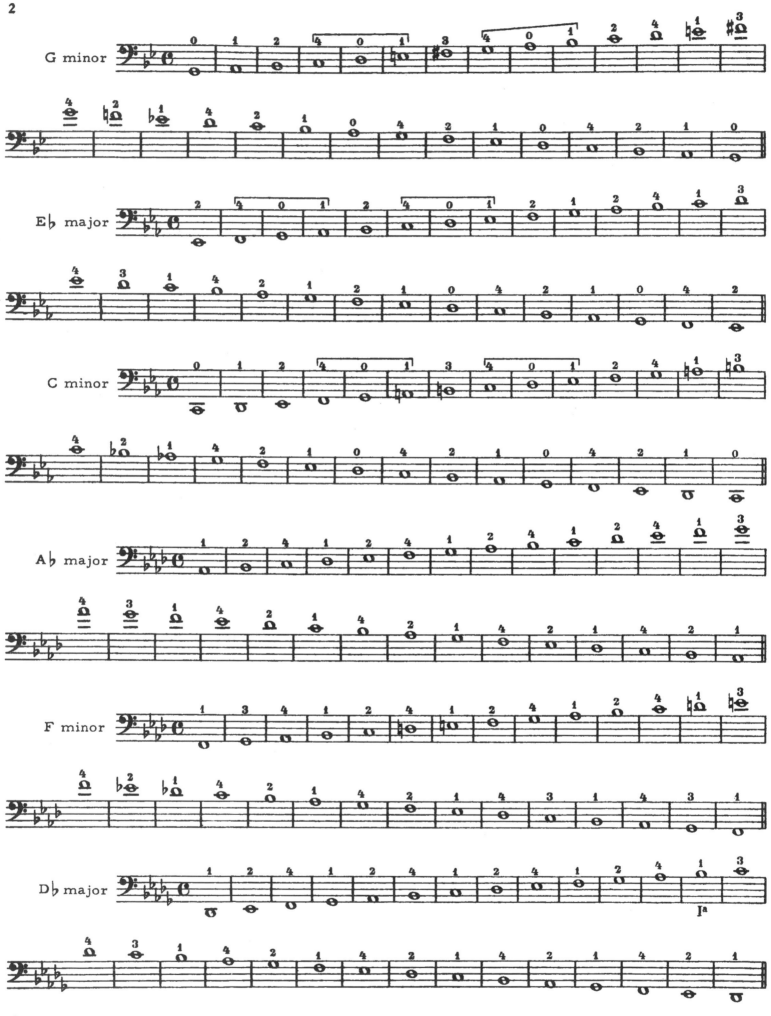

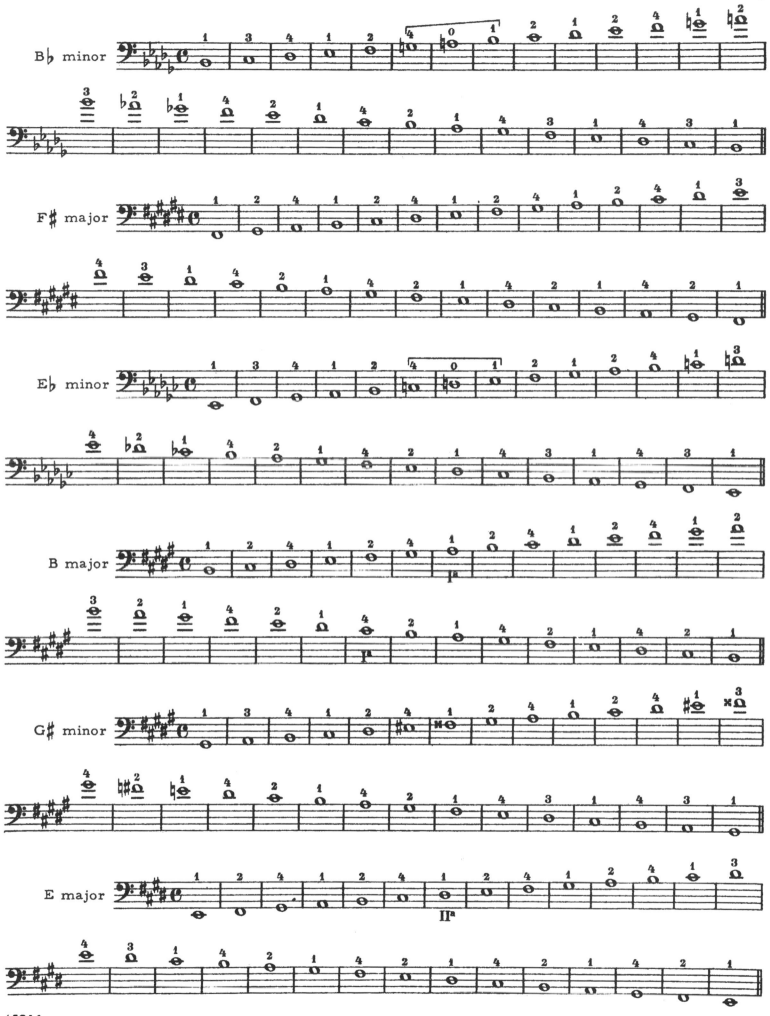

4

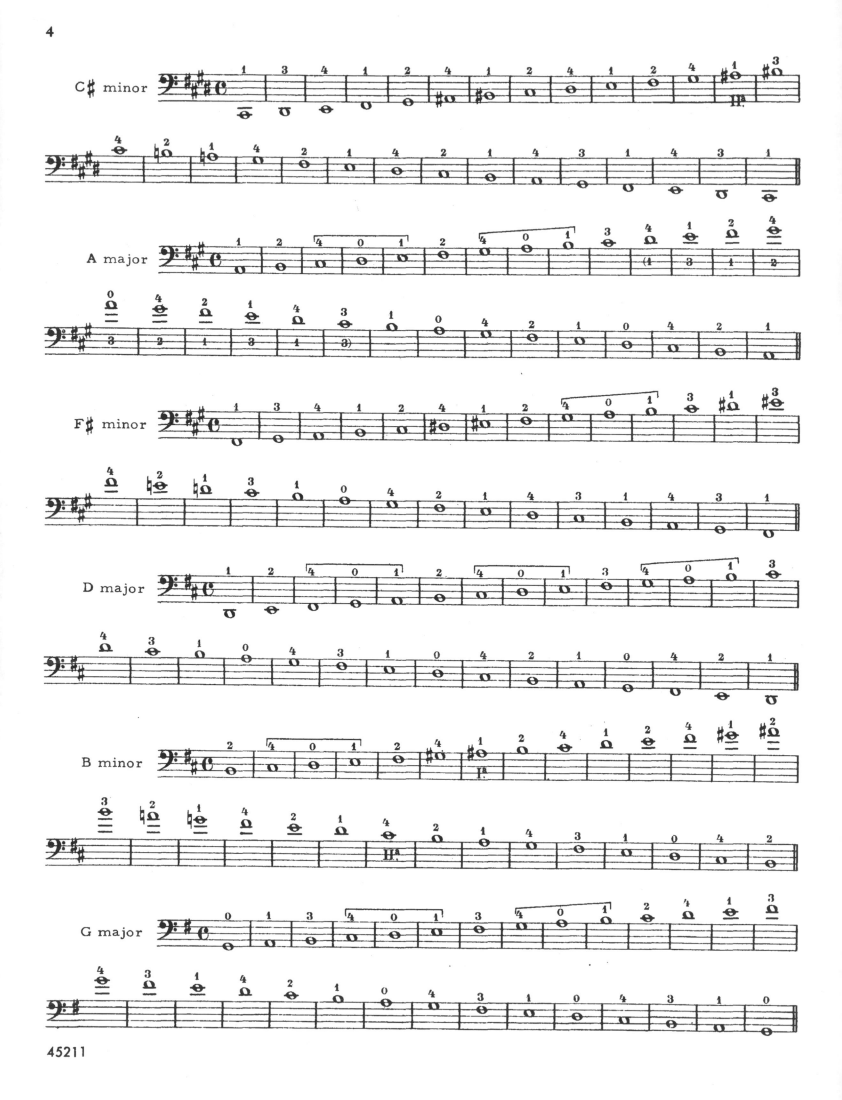

E minor

Bowings for scales of two octaves

8.

Triads through two octaves

Bowings for Triads through two octaves

Scales in thirds of two octaves (broken thirds)

Bowings for scales in thirds of two octaves

Scales in three octaves

Bowings for scales of three octaves

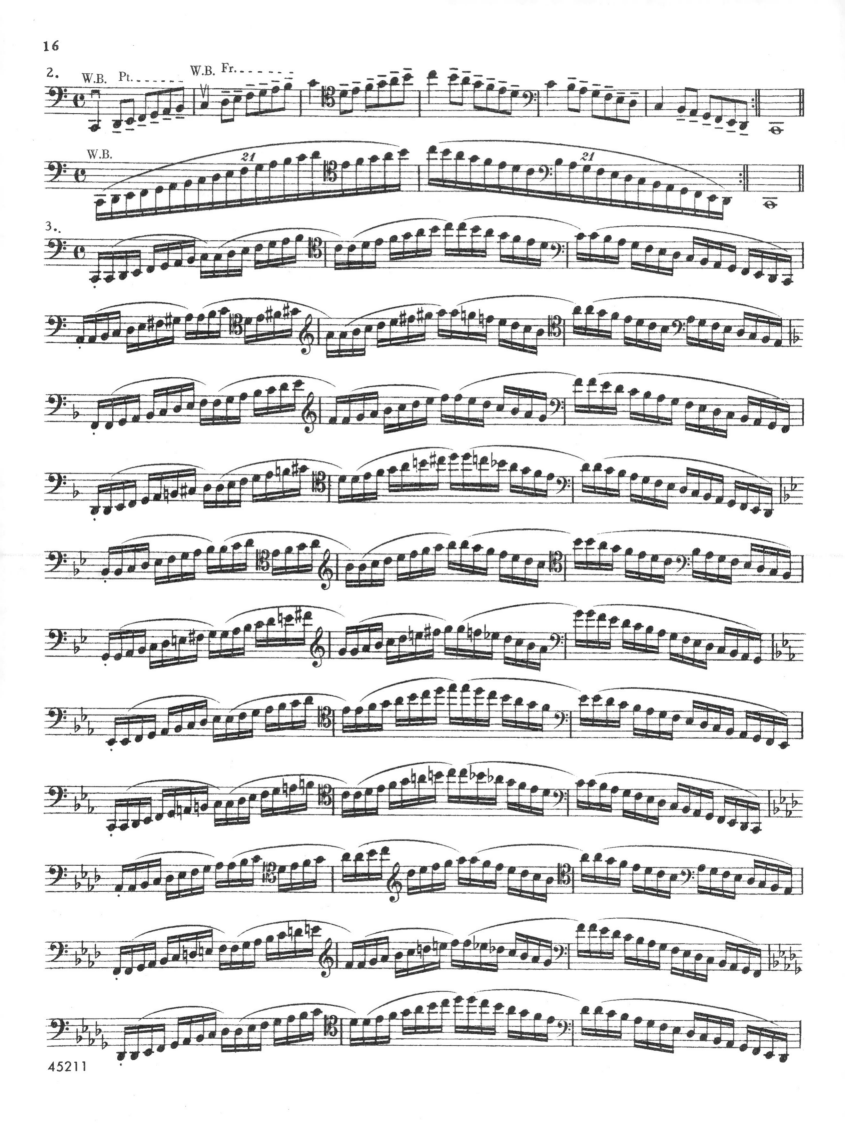

Triads through three octaves

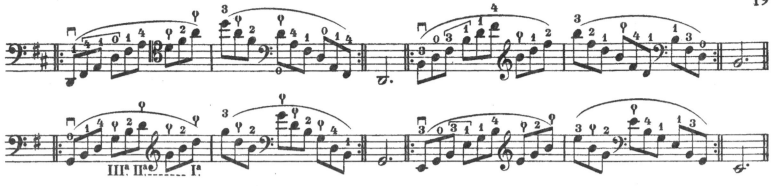

Bowings for Triads through three octaves

45211

Scales in thirds of three octaves

45211

24

45211

45211

26

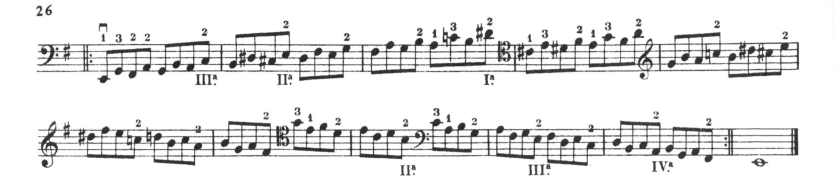

Bowings for scales in thirds of three octaves

Scales in four octaves

45211

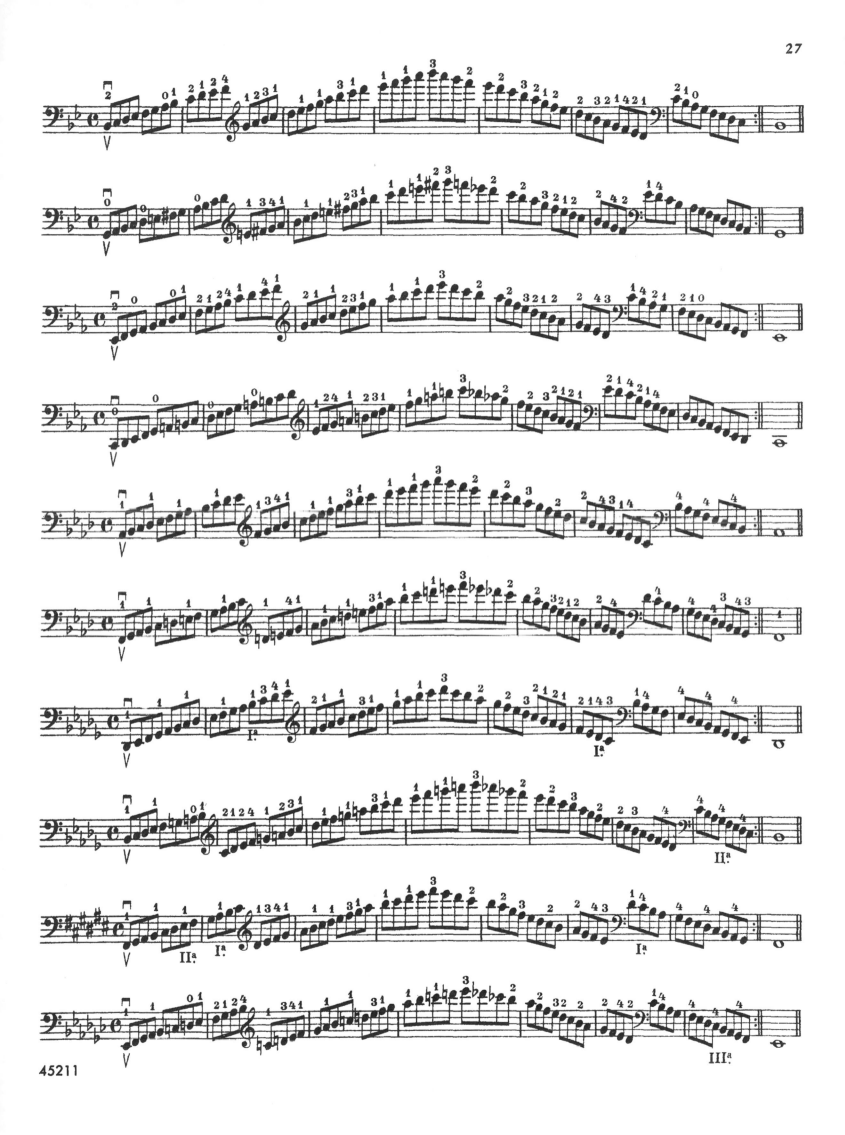

27

28

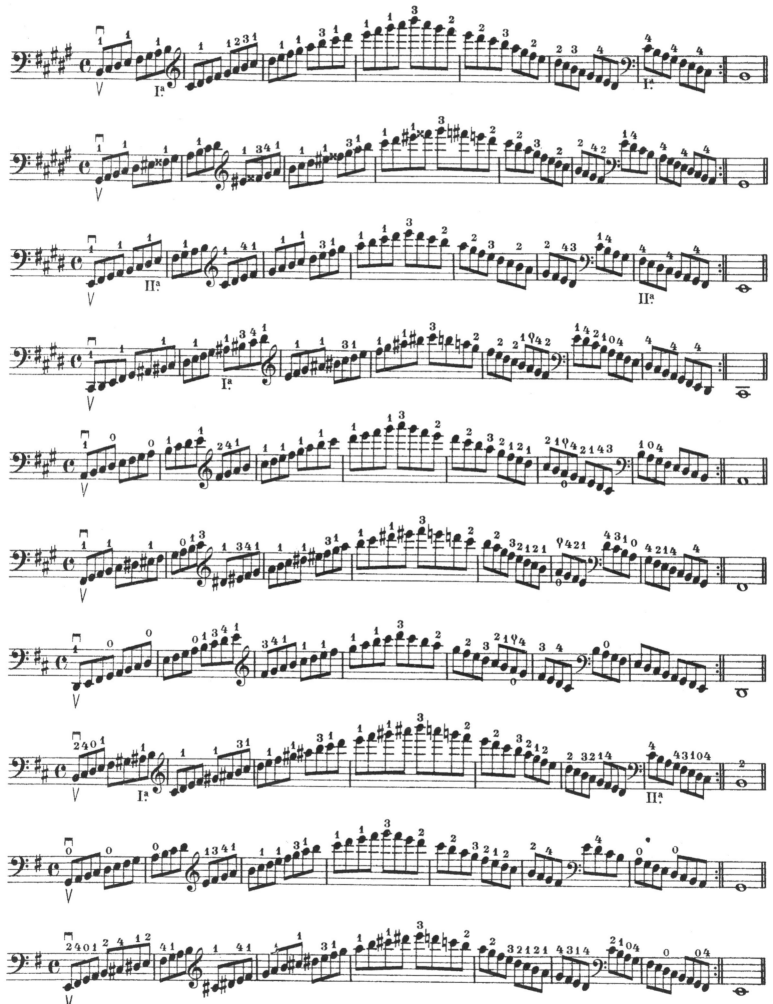

45211

Bowings for scales of four octaves

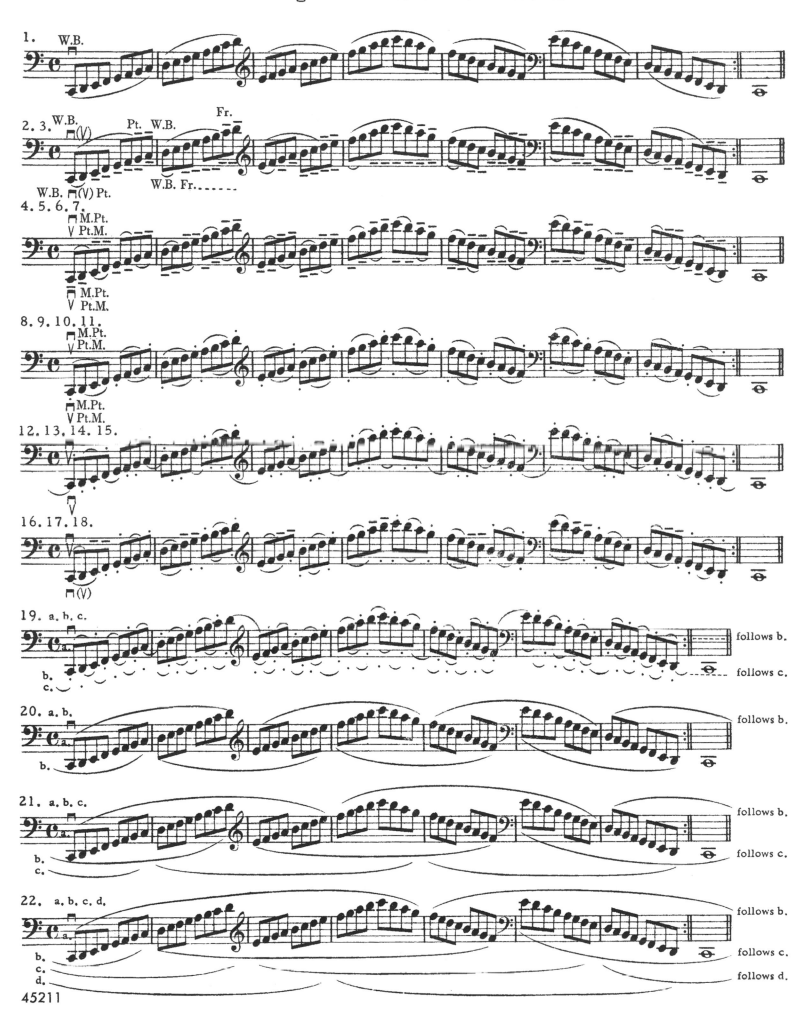

30. 31.

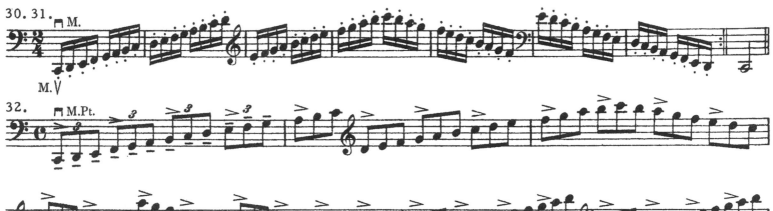

32.

33. 34. W.B. Pt.

35. 36.

37. 38.

39. 40.

45211

41.

Triads through four octaves

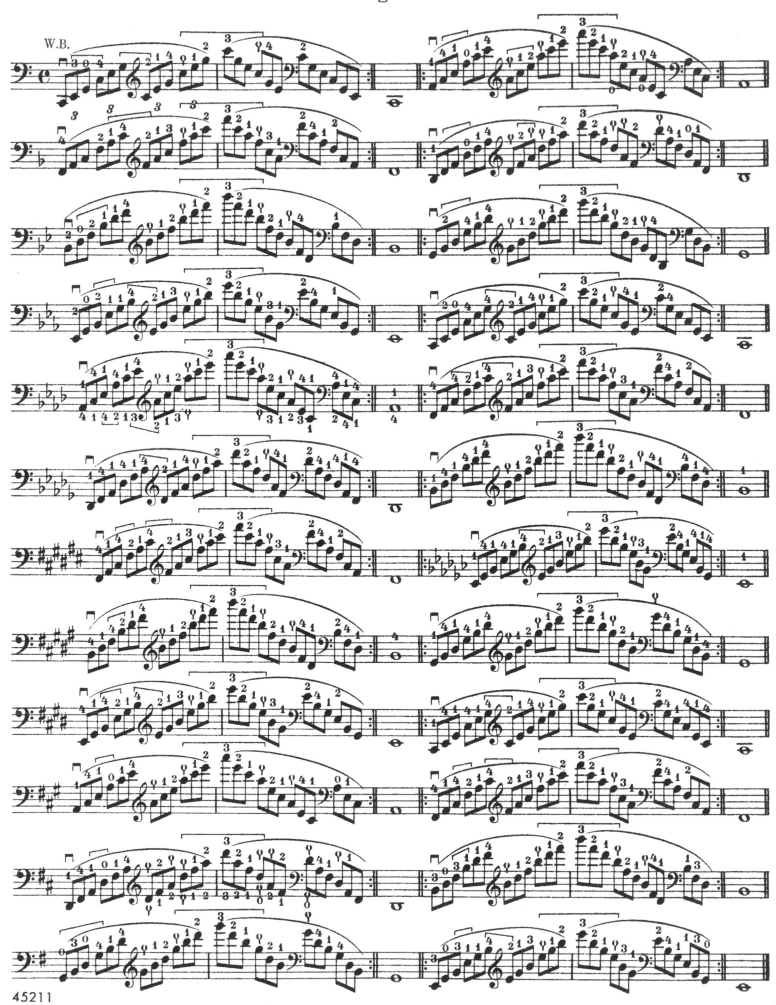

Bowings for Triads through four octaves

Scales in thirds of four octaves

Bowings for scales in thirds of four octaves

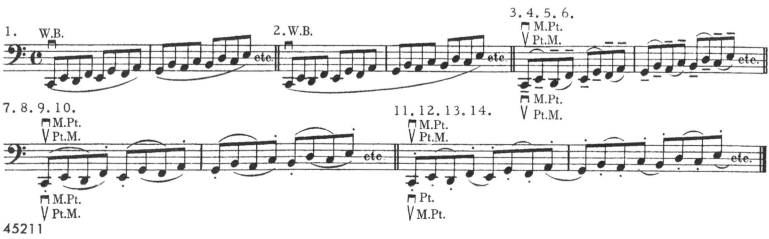